PURPOSEFUL RETIREMENT WORKBOOK & PLANNER

PURPOSEFUL RETIREMENT WORKBOOK & PLANNER

Wisdom, Planning, and Mindfulness
for Your Happiest Years

HYRUM SMITH

Mango Publishing
Coral Gables

For permission requests, please contact the publisher at:

Mango Publishing Group
2850 Douglas Road, 2nd Floor
Coral Gables, FL 33134 USA
info@mango.bz

For special orders, quantity sales, course adoptions and corporate sales, please email the publisher at sales@mango.bz. For trade and wholesale sales, please contact Ingram Publisher Services at customer.service@ingramcontent.com or +1.800.509.4887.

Purposeful Retirement Workbook & Planner: Wisdom, Planning, and Mindfulness for Your Happiest Years
Library of Congress Cataloging
ISBN: (print) 978-1-63353-812-2 (ebook) 978-1-63353-813-9
Library of Congress Control Number: 2018947011
BISAC category code: FAM005000—FAMILY & RELATIONSHIPS / Life Stages / Later Years

Printed in the United States of America

TABLE OF CONTENTS

PURPOSEFUL RETIRING

EXPLORING OPTIONS

DECIDING

PURPOSEFUL PLANNING

WEEKLY PLANNING & ACCOMPLISHMENTS

WELCOME TO
RETIREMENT!

Welcome to your time! No longer are you an unwilling subject to alarm clocks that ring too early, coworkers who act incompetently, and in-boxes that never stay empty. The day is yours to fill—or not to fill—as you choose. This is your time.

As amazing as that sounds, retirement can also be unsettling. It's simply an odd creation of a modern society. How do you go from daily, routine activity over a period of forty years or more to nothing just because you reached a certain age or a certain date on the calendar? How does it all just end?

A job ending can and should be an exciting personal beginning. This is your time! What are you going to do with it? Whatever you choose to do, don't focus on the "tire" part of retirement. This is not the time to tire out.

For decades you've made a difference in your home, in your community, in your office. You've made a difference at both a personal and professional level.

Don't stop now. I don't know about you, but I'm not going to let someone hand me a Social Security check and shoo me away. I am going to treat retirement as my time. I am going to ensure I make a difference with the time I am given.

"I will not go quietly."
—Don Henley

THE REST OF YOUR LIFE CAN BE THE BEST OF YOUR LIFE

The British have a saying, "Who is she when she's at home?" This idiom from across the pond points to something very important—we show different faces to the world. In recent decades, we spend more time at the office than anywhere. Thus, the face you show at work is very closely tied to your sense of self. Most of us spend around 50 years working, and whether you climbed the corporate ladder or spent your days at a trade you love, working-life is deeply encoded in your identity. There is also the social aspect, with friendships, rites of passage, shared goals, and close bonds from shared failures and successes. From your lunchtime chats over the years you no doubt know the names of your coworkers' children, spouses, and maybe even their pets. They, in turn, know about your hopes and dreams, have weathered your career setbacks alongside you and have been there for you through it all. Many lifelong friendships have started at the workplace, to be treasured and maintained long after the job ends.

It is not so easy to simply drop this side of you as you enter this new phase of your life. The best advice I can pass along is that you are still you. You bring the same value to the world even when you stop going to work five days a week. In fact, you might now be able to contribute more in service to the world by giving back to others, a marvelous benefit that comes with the opportunity to manage your time in a different way.

It's all in your hands, completely up to you. You have a choice, and my suggestion is that you embrace these years with zest. Whatever you do, do not withdraw from life or sit around and wait for things to happen. Be passionate, not passive. The rest of your life can be the best of your life. Each day is an opportunity to improve your relationships, stimulate your mind, invigorate your body, and grow spiritually. Retirement can easily be an unbelievably bright future for you and your loved ones. You are not a "has been," you are a "will be." Above all, be purposeful. Enjoy all that lies before you!

HOW TO USE THIS BOOK

This book isn't supposed to look pretty sitting on a table. This book is a tool for transforming your life. Write in it! Get it dirty! Use it for taking notes. Photocopy pages out of it. Try out your thoughts in the workbook sections. Experiment in the planning sections. Measure your progress by recording your thoughts and results in the weekly planning and accomplishment section.

Learn and grow.

PURPOSEFUL RETIRING

TURNING IN THE TITLE

We've all heard the stories. People facing immediate death never wish that they had spent more time at work. I believe these stories ring true because we all understand that we are more than a president, an accountant, an analyst, an assistant. We are more.

Being more does not end in retirement. In fact, retirement is the perfect time to add MORE to MORE. To leave a legacy.

Who are you? You are more than a fancy job title. You have value simply by being a human being. You've always had this value and you always will.

The danger comes when we allow ourselves to be defined by our job, our title, and the size of our paycheck. The danger comes when we ask, "When it is gone, what is left?" You are. You are left. You, with your skill, talent, and ability to make a difference. You. Who are you?

Life is full of changes. When we are no longer students, we adjust and change. When we choose to leave a career to raise a family, we adjust and change. When our last child leaves for college and we are left with an empty nest, we adjust and change. When we retire, it's one more change. What is exciting about this change?

You now have the opportunity to focus on the people and things that really matter!

NOW IT IS TIME FOR YOU TO FIND CLARITY

Research tells us that if we want to understand how we feel about something, we go a step beyond just thinking about it or even talking about it. We write it down. We choose the deadline. We define the steps to get there. Through writing we are able to gain clarity. Our jumbled thoughts find their order on the page.

Two camps. What camp are you in?

There are two retirement camps. Which one do you fall into? It has been my experience that in Camp One you'll find people who have been planning and looking forward to retirement since the day they started their first real job. As they have gotten closer to THE DAY, they've inserted a countdown as a screensaver on their work computer. And on the day they retire, they nearly dance out the door.

In Camp Two there are people who "do not go gentle into the good night." They go out the door kicking and screaming, their fingers tightly gripping the door jamb of their office because retirement looms before them like an empty abyss.

WHAT CAMP ARE YOU IN
WHAT THINGS DID YOU DO
TO PREPARE FOR THIS DAY?

WHAT DID RETIREMENT LOOK
LIKE FOR YOUR PARENTS?

WHAT DOES YOUR PARTNER ENVISION FOR YOUR RETIREMENT?

Ask your partner his or her thoughts.

WHAT DO YOU THINK RETIREMENT WILL LOOK LIKE FOR YOUR CHILDREN AND GRANDCHILDREN?

MY BELIEF WINDOW

You possess a Belief Window. Can you see it?
Can you touch it? No, but it is part of you.
It hangs right in front of your face.
When you move, it moves with you.

This Belief Window controls how you see the world because you see
everything through it. When you establish a personal belief, you write
it on your Belief Window.

Just because you write it, however, does not make it true. Over time
you accumulate thousands of beliefs on your Belief Window. Some
beliefs are true, some are not. Some are rational, some are not. But
what they all do is meet a need you have. You need to define the world
around you, and your Belief Window helps you do just that.

You might think all dentists like to inflict pain. You might think white
cars are easier to keep clean. You might think fountain drinks are
better than canned. We all have beliefs. And we all collect them on our
Belief Window.

What beliefs about retirement are on your Belief Window?

- Unemployed people are lazy
- Personal value only comes through hard work
- Important people have important titles
- If I'm busy, I'm important

How do my beliefs control the way I see retirement?

*"There is a fountain of youth: it is your mind, your talents, the creativity you bring to
your life and the lives of people you love. When you learn to tap this source, you will
truly have defeated age."*
—Sophia Loren

HOW DO I PERCEIVE RETIREMENT?

List your beliefs regarding retirement.

AVOID AWFULIZING YOUR RETIREMENT!

I came across a term the other day that made me stop for a minute and think. The term was "awfulizing retirement."
What does it mean to "awfulize retirement"? According to the author who coined it, Jonathan Looks, it means to think so much about the things that could go wrong that you're afraid to move forward. [1]

He wrote: When pondering retirement, many people fantasize about, say, life on the beach or having time to write the next great American novel or finally being able to spend more time with our grandchildren. But when action and decision-making are required, fear distorts the picture. Opportunity starts to look like a nightmare. The human brain is an amazing thing, but it doesn't deal with uncertainty very well.

Retirement is a bet on the future, and no one can anticipate all the unknowns. The data is necessarily incomplete. When confronted with incomplete data, our brains look at the information gaps and fills them with fear. To the brain, anything is better than ambiguity.

In our mind, the worst case scenarios suddenly become the most likely of circumstances. We begin to doubt our calculations. We begin to doubt the experts. At the very time we need to trust our judgment the most, fear gets into our head, distorts our outlook and overwhelms all our assumptions.

Hence the term psychologists use to define this phenomenon: *awfulizing*.

---

[1] https://www.forbes.com/sites/nextavenue/2017/06/23/how-i-stopped-awfulizing-retirement/#5759c171bafd

PLAN, THEN EMBRACE YOUR ADVENTURE!

How did Jonathan Looks overcome this state of awfulizing? He decided to pay more attention to his dreams and less attention to his fears.

I envisioned my dreams—of traveling the world, of enhancing my photography skills, and of learning about different cultures. I gave up on my need to know with certainty that my plans were the right ones. Instead, I wholeheartedly embraced the adventure.

Personally, I have found that when fear or stress or even panic attacks me, the worse thing I can do is to shove the feelings away and hope they do not come back. It always comes back. But if I think it through, I am telling my brain: "It's okay. There's a plan."

Eventually, your brain will realize there is no reason to keep bringing up these fears. There's a plan in place!

COMMON RETIREMENT FEARS

You may have some fears about retirement. Don't awfulize it. Plan.

Perhaps you're scared of:

- Living on a fixed income
- Losing your working identity
- Adapting to a new routine

You're not alone, but don't let the fear stop you from stepping into this new adventure. Author Mary Manin Morrissey shared, "Even though you may want to move forward in your life, you may have one foot on the brakes. In order to be free, we must learn how to let go… Release the fear."

Let's look at each fear individually and establish a plan that works for you!

*"Retirement is like a long vacation in Las Vegas.
The goal is to enjoy it to the fullest, but not so
fully that you run out of money."*

—Jonathan Clements

LIVING ON A
FIXED INCOME

One way to reduce the fear of living on a fixed income is to thoroughly plan. If you prefer, work with a retirement advisor to map out what your new budget may look like in retirement.

You may want to consider three basic elements:

- Needs
- Wants
- A Rainy Day Buffer

What those elements look like in a "normal" month will be different for everyone. A financial advisor should be able to examine your personal situation and provide recommendations.

NEEDS

Fear comes from the fact that you don't know what you don't know—until it's too late. So if you want to do some independent planning before you speak with a financial advisor, here are some thoughts:

- Housing. If you do not own your own home, you still have a mortgage to take care of every month. Remember to also include utilities (gas, electric, cable, internet, garbage, recycling, etc.) in this expense category.
- Medical Insurance. Depending on what type of medical insurance you have acquired for your retirement, chances are that you are still going to have to pay a monthly premium. Find out how much it is and do yourself a favor—plan for it to go higher.
- Additional doctor's visits. You'll need to plan for dentists visits and eye doctor visits.
- Taxes. This is a topic you want to discuss with a financial planner. How much should you expect to pay in taxes and is there any way to keep that amount as small as possible.
- Food! Food is a subject that can easily go in the Needs & Wants category. For now, think about how much you plan to spend for basic groceries. Fun nights out with friends at a restaurant can be addressed in the Wants category

List other needs that you should consider:

WANT

Time for fun.
This category is completely up to you. Fill it up by declaring to yourself, "I've waited decades to retire so that I could finally have time to _____."

Now, if you thought about a work project around the house, try again!

What would your retirement not be complete without?
And how much do you have to save to pay for it?

- Travel
- Weekly lunches with friends
- Extensive family visits
- Golf outings
- Spa memberships
- Deep sea fishing trips
- Season tickets to the theater or for your favorite sports team
- Cruises to exotic places

RAINY DAY BUFFER

What are those unavoidable expenses that inevitably pop up when least expected?

- *Prescriptions.* No matter your prescription drug plan, plan to have to pay for some things in the future out of pocket.
- *Home repairs.* Unfortunately, you and I are not the only things slowly breaking down! If you own your own home, how much longer is that washer going to last? How old is that air conditioning unit? Will you be able to pay to replace it when it breaks down?
- *Car repairs or replacement.* Most of us cannot live without the convenience of our always-available automobile. But, they break down and ultimately need to be replaced. For many of us, this can be an unexpected financial strain. You probably should plan for it.

LOSING YOUR WORKING IDENTITY

I remember speaking to a retired pilot at the conclusion of a presentation. Though he was retired, he still identified himself introduced himself as a retired American Airlines pilot.

"When they took those wings off my chest, something collapsed inside of me," he said. "I don't know who I am. I cannot tell people that I am a pilot anymore, and that is what I have felt, for decades, gave me value."

No matter what you did as a day job, your value comes from who you are, not what you did. Your value comes from who you are, and that's enough.

Writer Ginny Reynolds wrote for The Washington Post, "Retirees who seem to have no trouble going from working to not working did not identify themselves mostly by what they did for a living. Even if they did call themselves accountants or physicists, they no doubt also relied on other self-definitions."

Whether you realized it during your career or are realizing it more and more everyday:

You are more than your title!

ADAPTING TO A NEW ROUTINE

Your time is now your own. If you've hated your alarm clock for decades, go ahead and turn it off! But don't get rid of the alarm clock and grab a crocheted blanket and upgrade your recliner.

You may no longer have to do the things other people tell you to do. You are the Executive Manager of your own retirement. But there are still things you want to do! Time is a slippery thing. We may do something as simple as click on the television and we catch something interesting on a shopping channel and two hours later you find yourself a little poorer, with a little less of your day, and a new set of sheets that you didn't really need but the ladies on the television swore sleeping in them was like sleeping on a cloud. How could you turn that down?

If it's important to you, schedule it.

PURPOSEFUL HAPPINESS

In retirement, you mostly get to choose your own stress. Life in retirement is not going to be perfect. There are still things that you have to deal with. But now you're in charge of your own time. You are no longer compelled by a job and its responsibilities. While you are in control, while you are making choices, why not choose to be happy?

How can I choose happiness?

WHAT MAKES ME HAPPY?

- Reading books?
- Golfing with a friend?
- Lunch with a child or grandchild?
- Serving at a local theater or school?

Identify what makes you happy and put it into your retirement life.

In retirement you will need to set up new guidelines for productive days. Set goals, make to-do lists, figure out how to measure success outside of the workplace.

Ask yourself:
- What are other successful retirees doing?
- Are there lessons to be learned from them?
- What am I willing to do to have my own purposeful retirement?
- What expectations do I have of myself?
- How do I want to script my second act?

WHAT ARE YOU DOING
WHEN YOU FEEL THE HAPPIEST?

HAPPY ACTIVITY   WHY DOES IT MAKE ME HAPPY?

SOLO SENIORS

If you're retiring and single, you're in great company. A 2016 survey by the U.S. Census Bureau found that there were 19.5 million unmarried U.S. residents age 65 and older. If you are one of the nearly 20 million, you have slightly different concerns and slightly different adventures ahead of you.

First, the concerns.

BUILD YOUR RETIREMENT TEAM

There will come a time when you need some help. Plan ahead. You need a team —a community—to rely on when you physically or emotionally need someone else. Retirement is a great time to strengthen your team.

- Look to your extended family.
- Look to your friends.
- Who can you call when you feel sick and need help, whether it be picking up a prescription at the pharmacy or getting you some chicken noodle soup?
- And, how can you help others?

You may have a friend who is also a "solo senior" who needs a team, too. Reach out. Build a team. Make a difference in someone else's life and ensure something is there to make a difference in yours as well.

INNOCULATE YOURSELF AGAINST LONELINESS

You also need a team to ensure you do not sink into a pattern of isolation and loneliness. Recently I was speaking to a friend whose sister, only in her 70s, was suffering from agoraphobia. She had raised a family and had a successful career. But now she was refusing to leave her home because it scared her. In a matter of months she had experienced extreme weight loss and, in her brother's opinion, looked like she aged 20 years. She had gotten so used to her isolation she was literally scared of everything else.

Isolation and loneliness are not only emotional problems. It's an emotional problem with a physical consequence. Loneliness is believed to speed up the onset of dementia, lead to fatal heart disease, and contribute to an early death.

Which leads to our second point.

YOU HAVE WONDERFUL OPTIONS!

Being retired and single can be a great adventure and opportunity, and not just because you have sole possession of the remote control. The only person you have to compromise with is yourself!

Consider some of the options you have as a solo senior.

TAKE A CLASS!

We all check some dreams at the door when we enter the "real world" and everything that comes with our "real world job." Go get those dreams back. You'll keep your mind engaged, you'll gain new skills, and you'll meet people who share a common interest. If finances are a concern, there are a lot of wonderful free resources available on the Internet. My friend Kris wanted to take a watercolor class and even signed up. But the class was very full and she did not get much attention from her instructor. She stayed in the class—she loved the weekly interaction with this group—but then she would go home, get on YouTube.com, and picked up some additional pointers. It's a great time to learn!

VOLUNTEER!

More than ever, you are needed. Where do you love to be? If you love to be around children, volunteers are needed in the schools. If you love the theater, you can volunteer to be an usher. If people feel they are making a difference, they want to get out of bed in the morning.

People who volunteer have a higher level of self-esteem and overall well-being. They feel connected to the world around them. They benefit from a feeling of community and feel less lonely and isolated.

CHOOSE YOUR OWN ADVENTURE!

One of the best parts of being a solo senior is the ability to choose your own adventure and to live exactly where you want to live. Maybe you want to purchase an RV and park it in your child's driveway so that you can attend every soccer game, every dance recital of your grandchildren. Maybe you want to find a roommate and reenact scenes from The Golden Girls. Maybe you want to live in a retirement community that offers classes, shopping trips, game nights, and other social outings. Pick a maybe!

DON'T LIMIT YOURSELF!

There may be some adventures you don't want to take because you do not want to do it alone. Whether it be an outing to a movie or a trip to the Bahamas, you might want to go but decide you cannot go alone. If that's true, look for companions who will go with you. Plan outings! Plan trips! Whatever you do, get outside of your home and interact with the world around you. If you're willing to be brave, go on a trip by yourself. You can start small. You can go on a daytrip somewhere near you. You can build up to a weekend or a longer guided tour or cruise.

Just don't limit yourself!

EXPLORING OPTIONS

WHAT ARE MY OPTIONS?

Everyone has their own dream retirement. The difficulty is being brave enough to make that dream come true, whether it's fishing every day or seeing the world. You have been a responsible adult your whole life. Now you finally have the time and a world of options. What do you want to do? Time to have some fun and think about your options. Dream a little. What have you always wanted to do?

Go back and get that degree in philosophy if it's what you always wanted to do. Stop watching Top Chef on television and start taking culinary classes. Go to a local guitar shop and sign up for classes.

I am a big proponent of making an appointment with your spouse or partner. Sit down with each other. Talk. No cell phones, no iPads, just talking and planning together on a regular, scheduled basis. Be present with each other.

Write down something you would really like to do if time and money were not object. What do you want to do?

LET'S BRAINSTORM

- Start a new business (do it with a son or daughter, if possible)
- Become a political activist in your community
- Run for a political office
- Walk parts of the Appalachian trail or the Pacific Crest Trail
- Become a master photographer
- Downsize and build your retirement dream house
- Start up a continuing education program in your community
- Go on an African safari
- Organize a family reunion
- Form a book club
- Earn a Life Master in the American Contract Bridge League
- Write a book
- Start a blog or a YouTube video-sharing website
- Learn to dance
- Mentor a youth
- Learn to play a musical instrument
- Make a difference for a needy family
- Create and complete a book-reading bucket list
- Organize an investment club
- Raise a puppy
- Study great literature
- Learn a new word every day
- Learn to be a gourmet cook
- Learn a new language

- Study local history and visit the places you learn about
- Research your family history
- Read to older people at an assisted-living facility

The list is only limited by your imagination. Add some of your own brainstorming ideas here.

RETIREMENT SHOULD BE A GIFT THAT IS SHARED!

What's the earliest birthday you remember?

Do you remember the cake? The friends who celebrated with you?
The gifts you were given? How do those memories change as you reflect on the most recent
birthday you've celebrated? Were your thoughts still on the cake you had? The presents
you were given? Or does your mind reflect on the people you shared the day with and the
expressions of love you received? What have you learned about true gifts from that earliest
birthday to your most recent?

I want my older life to be about giving, not getting.

What can I give? Who do I want to give it to?

ALL THE WAYS RETIREMENT CAN BE A GIFT!

Since retirement is a gift, who can you share that gift with today?

Now is the time because now you have the time. Now is the time to launch a new career—
the one you always wanted but couldn't because you needed a predictable paycheck. Now is
the time to focus on your family. Now is the time to make a difference in your community.

*Is there a friend, grandchild, younger person
who needs your time?*

List what you want to give and to whom

What   **To Whom**

_____   _____
_____   _____
_____   _____
_____   _____
_____   _____
_____   _____
_____   _____
_____   _____
_____   _____
_____   _____
_____   _____
_____   _____
_____   _____
_____   _____
_____   _____
_____   _____
_____   _____
_____   _____
_____   _____

WHO DO YOU WANT TO SHARE-THE-GIFT-OF-RETIREMENT WITH?

- Partner
- Children
- Grandchildren
- Greater Family
- Friends
- Less Fortunate
- Pet
- Myself
- Community
- Country
- Planet

Use this page to explore the ways you can share your time with others.
List the people you do it with. How can you do so? Be specific!

HERE ARE SOME SHARE-THE-GIFT-OF-RETIREMENT IDEAS!

VOLUNTEERING

Within everyone is a desire to make a difference. Choosing to actively make a difference can change your whole retirement. If you feel you are making a difference, you simply become happier as a result. If you feel you are making a difference, you are excited to get out of bed in the morning. You may even live longer because you have something to live for. How can you make a difference? One way is to volunteer!

Try to earn all or some of these six badges:

7 Days of
Volunteer Work
at Local
Elementary School

7 Days of
Planning/Organizing
a Neighborhood Yard
Sale for Charity

7 Days of
Fostering a Pet
from the Shelter

7 Days of
Tutoring Students

7 Days of
Helping A Local
Youth Team By
Being An Assistant

7 Days of
Art by Volunteering
as a Docent

Brainstorm some volunteering ideas!

- Find a local community theater and volunteer as an usher or a stage hand
- Provide rides to the hospital or to the grocery store for someone in need
- Mentor a child at a local school or through your local library
- Serve meals at a homeless shelter
- Play music or sing at a retirement home
- Cut your neighbor's lawn
- Teach classes at a community center
- Repair a friend's car

GRANDCHILDREN

We tend to think a legacy needs to be something worthy of the front page of the newspaper. That's not right. Living an honest life is a legacy. Serving others is a legacy. No, it's not the front page of the newspaper. But, it's what really matters.

How about building a legacy with a grandchild? The closer the relationship between grandparent and the grandchild, the less likely either one is to develop depression. How do you define a "close relationship" or a " close bond"? Here's how many define a close relationship or bond:

- Grandchild feels emotionally close to the grandparent
- Grandchild has regular contact with the grandparent
- Grandchild sees the grandparent as a source of social support

If we want to communicate better and develop stronger relationships, we have to communicate both our way and their way. Our way may be a phone call, a handwritten letter, a text. What a treat that would be for a grandchild to find in the mailbox. Their way might be texting, tweeting, and getting on those social media sites. If you cover all your bases, you've done a great job.

Jot down some grandchild "relationship" ideas. Make a list of your grandchildren and determine what you can do for each one.

FRIENDS

Do you remember your first good friend? What made you friends? Did you live on the same block? Did you go to the same school? What did you do together?

What about as a young adult? Did you have one good friend that liked the same type of movies or the same pizza toppings?

And when your family and life ALMOST got too busy for friends, what friend did you hold onto? Why?

Friends are the family we get to choose.
They give us a sense of belonging. They share in our joy, they comfort us in sorrow, and they love us when we are simply unlovable.

You can form friendships around your service, around your hobbies, and around your interests.

- If you like to fly fish, take another retired person with you. Pick their brain and find new, interesting fishing holes.
- If you like to travel, find a friend and plan a trip together. And then actually take it.
- If you like to serve in your community, learn the names of the people around you. Be the first to welcome a new person in any setting.

List some ideas for forming new friendships that fit what you like to do.

MENTORING

I once spoke with a friend about a recent vacation she took into the mountains near her home. While driving along a dirt road, which like a lot of dirt roads we are familiar with do not lead to where we hoped, she saw a true movie star that she loved and admired. It was not someone who looked like this movie star. It was really him. This friend quickly realized that it all made sense since she heard this particular movie star owned property nearby.

She kept driving a little bit more before she realized it was time to admit defeat and turn around. Unfortunately, this movie star thought that my friend was in full-blown stalking mode. He walked over to her slow-moving car (it was a dirt road, after all), knocked on the window, and did not offer up directions or suggestions. Instead, he said, "Please, stop embarrassing yourself" and then he walked away. My friend was crushed.

That unfortunate day my friend lost someone she admired, but luckily not a mentor. You see, my friend may have a horrible sense of direction, but she understands that some relationships are real—ones that we have with friends, family, neighbors—and some are rather fake—like the ones we see on the movie screen but are unfortunately abrupt and rude in real life.

Look around and find someone you admire, someone ten or fifteen years older than you are. Ask them about their retirement.
- How is it going?
- What do you like about your retirement?
- What do you recommend doing?
- What do you wish you had done differently in your retirement, right from the start?
- How can you be fulfilled by something that has absolutely nothing to do with your past chosen career?

Who was your mentor growing up? What made them your mentor? For this exercise, the goal is to get the creative juices flowing. Find the writer in you and tell the story of your first mentor or mentors.
- Who were they?
- How did you meet?
- What did they teach you about life?
- What did they teach you about yourself?
- Have you passed down what they taught you to someone else?

Find your mentoring niche!

"Before you speak, listen. Before you write, think. Before you spend, earn. Before you invest, investigate. Before you criticize, wait. Before you pray, forgive. Before you quit, try. Before you retire, save. Before you die, give.."

—William A. Ward

MY FIRST MENTOR

EXPLORE HOW YOU CAN BE A MENTOR TO OTHERS.

What would be your mission?

MY MOST POWERFUL
PROFESSIONAL MENTOR

(If the same, ponder what qualities they have
that you would like to embody.)

HOW CAN I MENTOR TODAY?

YOUR PARTNER

Tell me your love story.

Actually, scratch that. Telling lasts only as long as the sound of your voice. Let's do this. Write down your love story.
- How did you first meet?
- Where was your first date?
- What led up to your first kiss?
- Were you nervous to "meet the parents?" How did it go?

Love stories are miracles. Finding one person that you love and they love you too. It's a miracle.

Now write down your love story.

RETIRING TOGETHER

The partnership you have before retirement is the partnership you will have after retirement, only amplified. In your retirement, you will reap what you have sown during your partnership. Have you worked together as a team? Or have your paths led away from each other more than they have come together?

- How will household responsibilities change with both of you at home?
- Is part-time work an option, part of the plan, or not part of the plan? If so, what would you want to do and why?
- Do either of you want to travel? If so, how often and at what cost? Where? Why?
- What activities do you or both of you plan to engage in? How will these activities be balanced?
- What activities can you do together to strengthen your relationship? What are both of your expectations regarding family activities?
- Do you plan to downsize your home, move into a retirement community, move into assisted living, or try to remain in your home forever?

Negotiating together:

1. Choose a good time to talk. If there is a decision to be made, try to talk about it in stress-free times. Make an appointment and keep the appointment! Set it now.
2. Give each other your full attention. Remove all distractions. Discuss the decision to be made and lay out the options.
3. Thoroughly discuss all options and perspectives.
4. Never give up and say, "I don't care!" You'll both end up miserable if you do. Unexpressed feelings never go away; they come back in different forms.
5. Choose a solution that works for both of you. What is the solution?

DESCRIBE YOUR PERFECT RETIREMENT RELATIONSHIP WITH YOUR PARTNER

MYSELF

Take care of yourself

Let me share with you one simple truth: your retirement will only be as amazing as your health. I can provide a million different suggestions on how to have a purposeful retirement, but your ability to fully actualize the retirement that you want is directly linked to how seriously you take care of yourself.

Organ Recitals

What can you do at the next organ recital? Have you been to a organ recital lately? I detest them, and personally I am invited to too many. Any given day, you can sit among your peers and a discussion of organs begins quietly, but then gains momentum. Which organ is acting up, which one has threatened to stop working, and which one is working overtime? Some people really get into their own organ recital.

Change the topic! Talk about what you're reading. Talk about what you saw on your walk around the block. Talk about the next vacation you are planning. Talk about anything else. We need to have something meaningful to do and talk about beyond what is on television and our last set of pains.

Alternatives to Organ Recitals

If you feel good, you have the opportunity to do good. So what does that mean? It means if I want to have a purposeful retirement, I have to feel well. It means I have to go out and move my body. Have you moved today? What exercise can you do tomorrow?

Here's a great goal: I want to support my body so that my body will support me throughout my retirement. How do you reach that goal?

Before you start any exercise regime, start with a check-up with your doctor. While there, mention that you want to start exercising. Ask for suggestions. Start slowly with achievable expectations, and set a few short-term goals.

For example:

- Today I am going to walk around the block.
- Tomorrow I am going to swim for five minutes.
- Today I am going to bike around the neighborhood.
- Tomorrow I am going to jog to the stop sign.
- Today I am going to sign up for a yoga class.
- Tomorrow I am going to find an experience, certified Tai Chi trainer.

Keep moving forward. But, most importantly, just keep moving.

WHAT CAN YOU DO TODAY TO IMPROVE HOW YOU ARE TAKING CARE OF YOURSELF?

DECIDING

WHAT DO YOU LOVE?

"Passion is energy.
Feel the power that comes from focusing on what excites you."
—Ophrah Winfrey

The other day I asked a young friend how his job was going.

"I love it," he said.

I admit, I was surprised. I knew it was his first job. And usually first jobs are far from exciting.

"Really?" I asked. "Where are you working?"

It turns out that he works in an office a few miles from home. In fact, on nice days he can ride his bike there. His days are full of scanning and filing. Like I assumed—far from exciting.

"Why do you like it?" I asked.

"My coworkers are great," he answered. "They think I'm rally smart. They ask me to help. They always say thank you. They talk about how I'll be running the company one day."

And I realized, he just might. Because of how he has been treated, this temporary employee just might stay forever.

LETS DO SOME SOUL-SEARCHING

Set aside fear and duty. Plan to do what you love to do. When we act out of love, miracles happen.

1. What do you love to do?
2. What is fun to you?
3. What do you want to do?
4. What gives you a sense of fulfillment and satisfaction?

I LOVE...

DO SOMETHING NEW

So do something, especially something new. If you can only talk about what you previously did in your life from your job, it means that you are not doing anything new. You're not living.

Retirement should be about doing something new, but also something you love. Ask yourself some probing questions:

1. What do you feel passionate about doing?
2. What brings you joy?

DO SOMETHING OLD AND MAKE IT NEW

Remember what you loved most about your last day job and find a way to make it fit into your new life.

- Besides getting paid, what did you like about your day job?
- What skills, talents, and business contacts can you take with you?

Loved most   *Why*

WHAT DID I LEAVE BEHIND?

What did you leave behind in your childhood in order to be a more responsible adult?

- Were you too busy to practice the piano?
- Did your easel and art supplies collect dust or dry up in the back of the closet?
- Did you put your bike into rental storage with just happy memories of riding for miles?

Well, tune the piano. Set up the easel.
Get the bike out of storage.

WHAT DID I LEAVE BEHIND?

IF TIME AND MONEY WERE NO OBJECT, I WOULD VISIT...

IF TIME AND MONEY WERE NO OBJECT, I WOULD LEARN TO...

IF TIME AND MONEY WERE NO OBJECT, I WOULD RECONNECT WITH...

WHAT CAN I DO TO MAKE A DIFFERENCE?

You can decide to make a difference. You can decide, "Today, I'm going to contribute!" Today I am going to:

- Help my daughter paint her living room.
- Pick up trash at my local park.
- Participate in community gardening.
- Teach art classes at my local elementary school.
- Read books to children in the hospital.

"Today I am going to be involved in something that matters!" And, friends will follow from your service. Friends are always a byproduct of serving.

SO NOW IT'S YOUR TURN TO MAKE A DREAM POSSIBILITIES LIST!

Whether your dream is to start your dream career, travel to some or all of those wonderful dream destinations, to give the gift of your retirement time to your community, or all of the above, the basic steps to achieving your dreams are exactly the same. Write down your dream and start planning for it right now! So, take the first step toward your purposeful retirement future.

List your dream possibilities
Don't worry about whether you think they're achievable or not – just list them!

MY DREAM POSSIBILITIES LIST

NOW LET'S NARROW THE LIST DOWN TO WHAT'S REALLY IMPORTANT TO YOU!

Things I really *want to do*

Things I maybe *want to do*

Things I never *want to do*

I-BEAM SOUL-SEARCHING EXERCISE

For decades I have shared what I refer to as the "I-Beam Experience." I invite people to visualize an I-Beam used in constructing skyscrapers.

Today it's your turn to go through the "I-Beam Experience." Imagine this I-Beam, about three hundred feet long, laying on the ground. You're at one end, and I am at the other. I shout out that I have one hundred dollars for you if you simply walk on this I-Beam over to me—the full three hundred feet.

Now, the I-Beam is safely on the ground so you can see that if you fall, it really would only be a very short distance. Chances are, you'd give it a try for one hundred dollars.

Now let's change things a little bit. I'm going to put that I-Beam on a truck and drive it to the Grand Canyon. I'm going to place it at the North Rim where there's a chasm about three hundred feet wide. The chasm is deep. In fact, it's over one thousand feet, straight down. The I-Beam is a little bowed. And did I mention that it is raining? And the wind gusts are nearly fifty miles per hour?

You're at one side, and I am on the other. The I-Beam stretches between us. I shout out an offer: "Cross the I-Beam and I will pay you one hundred dollars!" Would you cross?

Like I mentioned, I've taught this for decades. And for decades I've received the same answer: "No!" Not even when I raised the amount to one thousand dollars—ten thousand dollars—one hundred thousand dollars! You get the point.

So let's change the situation again. We're still at the Grand Canyon. There's still an I-Beam over a huge chasm. It's still raining. The wind is still howling. But I'm no longer a nice guy holding unmarked bills. I'm a horrible person, and I have ahold of your child or your grandchild, and the only way to save your loved one is to walk that I-Beam, to cross the chasm.

Chances are, you'd be willing to take that walk.

IDENTIFY MY GOVERNING VALUES OR—WHAT MATTERS MOST

What value, idea, principle, or person has such great value to you that you would take that risk? What would you cross the I-Beam for?

Have you ever stopped and listened to the highest priorities in your life? If you did stop right now to make such a list, at the top of the paper you would write "Governing Values." Governing Values answer the question, "What are the highest priorities in my life?" When you live purposefully, they govern how you live your life.

When you prioritize your governing values, when you recognize those things in life that you would cross an I-Beam for, you have created your own *personal constitution*. Whether it's love, honesty, education, or health, these are things you will never compromise on.
This is what matters most!

ASK YOURSELF

- Does my management of time reflect my governing values?
- Am I giving the most time to that which matters the most?
- What can I do tomorrow to ensure that my time aligns with my priorities?

NOW, PUT YOURSELF ON THE I-BEAM ABOVE THE GRAND CANYON.

Who or what would you cross the I-beam for?

My Personal Constitution (What I would cross the I-beam for)

Bookmark this page.
You will want to refer it for later.

OTHER DECISIONS TO CONSIDER:

Control your own future by making other important decisions today. And, once you make your decisions, share them with those around you.

I believe that one of the things we fear most as we get older is losing control. Picturing a day when we surrender control of where we live, what (or if) we drive, and even what we eat is a frightening thing.

The other day I met a man who woke up on his ninetieth birthday, went outside, and mowed his lawn. Because he could! Because he was ninety years old and still in control.

Even if you are feeling great today, recognize that one day you may need help with your daily living. Take time now—while you're feeling great—to make decisions for a time when you may not.

Take control over your future by making a decisions today. You have many decisions to make.

Do you foresee a time when you give a Power of Attorney to an adult child?

Do you have any specific end of life wishes? For example, do you need to file a Do Not Resuscitate order? Have you written a will or estalished a trust?

What are your long-term health wishes?

Notes

WHAT DECISIONS HAVE YOU ALREADY MADE TO MAINTAIN CONTROL OF YOUR RETIREMENT?

WHAT DECISIONS DO YOU STILL HAVE TO MAKE?

WHEN WILL YOU MAKE THE DECISION? WHEN CAN YOU START THE PROCESS?

WHO NEEDS TO BE
PART OF THIS DISCUSSION?

PURPOSEFUL PLANNING

THE NEED FOR PLANNING DOES NOT STOP WHEN YOU RETIRE

You just now have more time to play with. There is more time within your control. What do you want to do with it?

If your great-grandfather missed his stagecoach, what did he do? He might have tried to catch up to it or wait until the next one ventured through. If you grandmother missed her train, what did she do? She probably waited for the next one. If my father missed an airplane, he probably asked for help getting a seat on the next one. If you and I are temporarily stopped by a red light, we curse the traffic gods as we wait the two minutes for the light to turn green again. What has happened to us? We're time locked.

How can you make time work for you and not against you?

SCHEDULES AND LIVING IN LINE WITH MY VALUES

Why are schedules valuable tools? Because they bring our priorities to the forefront. They ensure that our actions match our values. For example, if you say that you value your health but you do not spend any time being active during the day, your actions do not match your values.

An hourly schedule is an opportunity to get really clear about what you are going to do and when you are going to do it. If you take it seriously, if you stick to it, you'll be able to more fully live in line with your values.

And remember to make time to try new things. If the stories you tell others are only about what you used to do, you're no longer living. You're just remembering.

MY TWENTY-FOUR HOURS

We all have twenty-four hours. Just twenty-four. I have the same amount of time that you have, that Warren Buffet has – even Bill Gates has twenty-four hours.

Everyone is given twenty-four hours. What are you going to do with yours? Will you reach out to a friend? Will you take a walk with someone you love? Will you play a game with someone who desperately needs your attention? Will you paint? Write? Travel?

Whatever it is, choose what makes you happy. Choose something that makes you feel fulfilled, like you are making a real difference. Choose something that will bring joy and purpose into your retirement and all of your twenty-four hours.

What do you want to control in your twenty-four hours?

LET'S LOOK AT YOUR TWENTY-FOUR HOURS YESTERDAY.

List everything you did during those twenty-four hours

WHAT WAS PRODUCTIVE YESTERDAY?

When you act proactively, you are looking ahead. You are planning. Your are taking control of your time and, to a great extent, your life. When you are reactive, the world feels chaotic and you feel powerless. You are simply responding to what happens to you. You are choosing to be a victim.

Let's not be a victim of busyness.

Yesterday — What was *busy?*
What was *proactive?*

Busy   *Proactive*

YOU CAN MAKE WHAT WAS PROACTIVE YESTERDAY A GOAL

What are the *steps* to a proactive goal?
What is your *schedule* for accomplishing
these steps?

Goal   *Steps*   *Schedule*

Goal   *Steps*   *Schedule*

Goal   *Steps*   *Schedule*

_____   _____
_____   _____
_____   _____
_____   _____
_____   _____
_____   _____

Goal   *Steps*   *Schedule*

_____   _____
_____   _____
_____   _____
_____   _____
_____   _____
_____   _____

Goal   *Steps*   *Schedule*

_____   _____
_____   _____
_____   _____
_____   _____
_____   _____
_____   _____

THE PERFECT RETIREMENT DAY

Think about the perfect hourly plan for tomorrow. What things, activities, and goals do you want in your day? What is my perfect breakfast? Perfect friends? Perfect weather? Perfect location?

What sequence of events are you choosing to put into your day? It doesn't matter what you choose to do, as long as it's proactive.

- Read a book
- Go for a run
- Have lunch with a friend
- Play golf with your brother
- Take a water aerobics class
- Help at your local food bank

Choose to do something that will give you a reason to get out of bed in the morning.

Choose to do something that will put some space between you and your recliner.

Choose to do something that will give purpose to your retirement.

HAVE I MADE
A DIFFERENCE?

Think about how daily planning can help you be more *proactive* in your retirement. Again, how can you stop being busy and start being proactive?

Now, begin drafting a daily plan of proactive goals for tomorrow. Make it your perfect retirement day.
Go beyond asking yourself:
- What am I going to do today?
- Go deeper and ask: *How am I going to make a difference?*

Proactive Goal	*How it makes a difference*

"I am not a product of my circumstances. I am a product of my decisions."
—Stephen R. Covey

MY IDEAL RETIREMENT BUCKET LIST

Create a detailed list of the activities, things, and goals that make up your ideal retirement. Be very specific.

Take a yellow marker and *highlight your priorities.*

MY PERFECT RETIREMENT DAY

Now, use your ideal retirement bucket list and create that perfect retirement day.

Perfect Retirement Day

6 AM

7 AM

8 AM

9 AM

10 AM

11 AM

12 PM

1 PM

2 PM

3 PM

4 PM

5 PM

6 PM

7 PM

8 PM

9 PM

10 PM

PERFECT RETIREMENT DAY TEMPLATE

One approach to scheduling is to turn your perfect retirement day into a template that can be adjusted as you see fit and/or cloned into a number of variations.

Template #1

6 AM	Awaken: Between 6 to 7 am
7 AM	Exercise: Walk the dog (1/2 mile route)
8 AM	Breakfast: Eat with spouse & catch up & discuss world events
9 AM	Goal: New Business Venture
10 AM	Goal: New Business Venture
11 AM	Goal: New Business Venture
12 PM	Lunch: (solo)
1 PM	Exercise: Walk the dog (1 mile route)
2 PM	Goal: New Business Venture
3 PM	Goal: New Business Venture
4 PM	Goal: New Business Venture
5 PM	Cocktail Hour: With Spouse & dog
6 PM	Dinner: Team with spouse on dinner preparation
7 PM	Activity: Walk with Spouse
8 PM	Activity: Facetime with Grandkids
9 PM	Activity: Read
10 PM	Bedtime: Between 10 to 11pm

PERFECT RETIREMENT DAY TEMPLATE

Template # _____

6 AM

7 AM

8 AM

9 AM

10 AM

11 AM

12 PM

1 PM

2 PM

3 PM

4 PM

5 PM

6 PM

7 PM

8 PM

9 PM

10 PM

PERFECT RETIREMENT DAY TEMPLATE

Template # _____

6 AM

7 AM

8 AM

9 AM

10 AM

11 AM

12 PM

1 PM

2 PM

3 PM

4 PM

5 PM

6 PM

7 PM

8 PM

9 PM

10 PM

PERFECT RETIREMENT DAY TEMPLATE

Template # _____

6 AM

7 AM

8 AM

9 AM

10 AM

11 AM

12 PM

1 PM

2 PM

3 PM

4 PM

5 PM

6 PM

7 PM

8 PM

9 PM

10 PM

PERFECT RETIREMENT DAY TEMPLATE

Template # _____

6 AM

7 AM

8 AM

9 AM

10 AM

11 AM

12 PM

1 PM

2 PM

3 PM

4 PM

5 PM

6 PM

7 PM

8 PM

9 PM

10 PM

PERFECT RETIREMENT DAY TEMPLATE

Template # _____

6 AM

7 AM

8 AM

9 AM

10 AM

11 AM

12 PM

1 PM

2 PM

3 PM

4 PM

5 PM

6 PM

7 PM

8 PM

9 PM

10 PM

WEEKLY PLANNING

& ACCOMPLISHMENTS

WEEKLY PLANNING

Have you ever looked back at your day and wondered, what exactly did I accomplish today? We've all had days when time seemed to get away from us. That's alright. Sometimes we desperately need those days. But what we don't want is for those days to become weeks or months or even years.

This is your retirement. Your time. Make it the best time. All it takes is a little preparation.

What do you want to do tomorrow? What do you want to do next week?

"Half our life is spent trying to find something to do with the time we have rushed through life trying to save."
—Will Rogers

PLAN FOR THE WEEK

The remainder of this book is your space for actually planning and accomplishing. You do not have to plan every minute of every day. In fact, don't even think about doing that because there's not enough space here!

Pick two or three things you'd like to get out of your day, write them down, and make them happen! Choose your Big Rocks--the things that are most important to you, time with a loved one, service, commitments; then fill in the things that are less important.

If you want to try the "template" approach, the next page provides an example of how it could be used. But, maybe you're more comfortable with your own way of doing things. That's great. Do what works for you.

But, write it down and get started!

PLAN FOR THE WEEK OF _09/23_ TO _09/29_

Monday

Use Template #1 (No changes)

NOTES

- Remember spouse's birthday
- Lunch date w/ Terry & Pat

Tuesday

Template #1 variations:
12PM: Lunch w/ Spouse
4PM: Mentoring meeting
6:30PM: Dinner w/ friends

Wednesday

Template #1 variations: 9PM: Read
12PM: Lunch (solo)
4PM: Gym
6PM: Team w/ Spouse on prep & I wash dishes

Thursday

Template #1 variations:
12PM: Lunch (w/ Terry & Pat to plan hike)
4PM: Cut lawn
6:30PM: (all evening) Spouse's birthday dinner

Friday

Template #1 variations:
12PM: Lunch (solo)
4PM: Continuing education meeting
7PM: Help spouse with computer skills

Saturday

Template #1 variations:
9AM: Gym
10-11AM: Household chores
12PM: Lunch (w/ spouse)

Sunday

Template #1 variations:
9-11AM: Household chores
12:30 (all afternoon): Boating & lunch w/ friends

ACCOMPLISHMENTS
FOR THE WEEK OF _____ TO _____

Monday

Made some vacation decisions with spouse during breakfast.
Worked out better quality control process for our new business.

Tuesday

Great mentoring meeting - scheduled follow up

Wednesday

Choose a hiking trail that agrees with both Terry and Pat

Thursday

Recruited two new members to help in setting up a continuing
education program

Friday

Fixed the railing on the deck

Saturday

Sunday

"Aging is not 'lost youth,' but a new stage of opportunity and strength."
—Betty Friedan

PLAN FOR THE WEEK OF _____ TO _____

Monday

NOTES

Tuesday

Wednesday

Thursday

Friday

Saturday

Sunday

ACCOMPLISHMENTS
FOR THE WEEK OF _____ TO _____

Monday

NOTES

Tuesday

Wednesday

Thursday

Friday

Saturday

Sunday

"The most effective way to do it, is to do it."
—Amelia Earhart

PLAN FOR THE WEEK OF _____ TO _____

Monday

Tuesday

Wednesday

Thursday

Friday

Saturday

Sunday

NOTES

ACCOMPLISHMENTS
FOR THE WEEK OF _____ TO _____

Monday

NOTES

Tuesday

Wednesday

Thursday

Friday

Saturday

Sunday

"I choose to make the rest of my life the best of my life."
—Louise Hay

PLAN FOR THE WEEK OF _____ TO _____

Monday

Tuesday

Wednesday

Thursday

Friday

Saturday

Sunday

NOTES

ACCOMPLISHMENTS
FOR THE WEEK OF _____ TO _____

Monday

NOTES

Tuesday

Wednesday

Thursday

Friday

Saturday

Sunday

"What you seek is seeking you."
—Rumi

PLAN FOR THE WEEK OF _____ TO _____

Monday

NOTES

Tuesday

Wednesday

Thursday

Friday

Saturday

Sunday

ACCOMPLISHMENTS
FOR THE WEEK OF _____ TO _____

Monday

NOTES

Tuesday

Wednesday

Thursday

Friday

Saturday

Sunday

"You know you're in love when you can't fall asleep because reality is finally better than your dreams."
—Dr. Seuss

PLAN FOR THE WEEK OF _____ TO _____

Monday

NOTES

Tuesday

Wednesday

Thursday

Friday

Saturday

Sunday

ACCOMPLISHMENTS
FOR THE WEEK OF _____ TO _____

Monday

Tuesday

Wednesday

Thursday

Friday

Saturday

Sunday

"Devote today to something so daring even you can't believe you're doing it."
—Oprah Winfrey

PLAN FOR THE WEEK OF _____ TO _____

Monday

NOTES

Tuesday

Wednesday

Thursday

Friday

Saturday

Sunday

ACCOMPLISHMENTS
FOR THE WEEK OF _____ TO _____

Monday

NOTES

Tuesday

Wednesday

Thursday

Friday

Saturday

Sunday

"The language of friendship is not words, but meanings."
—Henry David Thoreau

PLAN FOR THE WEEK OF _____ TO _____

Monday

NOTES

Tuesday

Wednesday

Thursday

Friday

Saturday

Sunday

ACCOMPLISHMENTS
FOR THE WEEK OF _____ TO _____

Monday

NOTES

Tuesday

Wednesday

Thursday

Friday

Saturday

Sunday

"I am always busy, which is perhaps the chief reason why I am always well."
—Elizabeth Cady Stanton

PLAN FOR THE WEEK OF _____ TO _____

Monday

Tuesday

Wednesday

Thursday

Friday

Saturday

Sunday

NOTES

ACCOMPLISHMENTS
FOR THE WEEK OF _____ TO _____

Monday

NOTES

Tuesday

Wednesday

Thursday

Friday

Saturday

Sunday

"The best way a mentor can prepare another leader is to expose him or her to other great people."
—John C. Maxwell

PLAN FOR THE WEEK OF _____ TO _____

Monday

Tuesday

Wednesday

Thursday

Friday

Saturday

Sunday

NOTES

ACCOMPLISHMENTS
FOR THE WEEK OF _____ TO _____

Monday

Tuesday

Wednesday

Thursday

Friday

Saturday

Sunday

"It's not how much we give but how much love we put into giving."
—Mother Teresa

121

PLAN FOR THE WEEK OF _____ TO _____

Monday

Tuesday

Wednesday

Thursday

Friday

Saturday

Sunday

NOTES

ACCOMPLISHMENTS
FOR THE WEEK OF _____ TO _____

Monday

Tuesday

Wednesday

Thursday

Friday

Saturday

Sunday

"No legacy is as rich as honesty."
—William Shakespeare

PLAN FOR THE WEEK OF _____ TO _____

Monday

NOTES

Tuesday

Wednesday

Thursday

Friday

Saturday

Sunday

ACCOMPLISHMENTS
FOR THE WEEK OF _____ TO _____

Monday

NOTES

Tuesday

Wednesday

Thursday

Friday

Saturday

Sunday

"If you're not making mistakes, then you're not making decisions."
—Catherine Cook

PLAN FOR THE WEEK OF _____ TO _____

Monday

NOTES

Tuesday

Wednesday

Thursday

Friday

Saturday

Sunday

ACCOMPLISHMENTS
FOR THE WEEK OF _____ TO _____

Monday

Tuesday

Wednesday

Thursday

Friday

Saturday

Sunday

"You can waste your lives drawing lines. Or you can live your life crossing them."
—Shonda Rhimes

PLAN FOR THE WEEK OF _____ TO _____

Monday

NOTES

Tuesday

Wednesday

Thursday

Friday

Saturday

Sunday

ACCOMPLISHMENTS
FOR THE WEEK OF _____ TO _____

Monday

NOTES

Tuesday

Wednesday

Thursday

Friday

Saturday

Sunday

"Do what you are afraid to do."
—Mary Emerson

PLAN FOR THE WEEK OF _____ TO _____

Monday

NOTES

Tuesday

Wednesday

Thursday

Friday

Saturday

Sunday

ACCOMPLISHMENTS
FOR THE WEEK OF _____ TO _____

Monday

NOTES

Tuesday

Wednesday

Thursday

Friday

Saturday

Sunday

"Passion is energy. Feel the power that comes from focusing on what excites you."
—Oprah Winfrey

PLAN FOR THE WEEK OF _____ TO _____

Monday

NOTES

Tuesday

Wednesday

Thursday

Friday

Saturday

Sunday

ACCOMPLISHMENTS
FOR THE WEEK OF _____ TO _____

Monday

NOTES

Tuesday

Wednesday

Thursday

Friday

Saturday

Sunday

*"Physical fitness is not only one of the most important keys to a healthy body,
it is the basis of dynamic and creative intellectual activity."*
—Henry David Thoreau

PLAN FOR THE WEEK OF _____ TO _____

Monday

NOTES

Tuesday

Wednesday

Thursday

Friday

Saturday

Sunday

ACCOMPLISHMENTS
FOR THE WEEK OF _____ TO _____

Monday

NOTES

Tuesday

Wednesday

Thursday

Friday

Saturday

Sunday

"Learn to value yourself, which means: fight for your happiness."
—Ayn Rand

PLAN FOR THE WEEK OF _____ TO _____

Monday

Tuesday

Wednesday

Thursday

Friday

Saturday

Sunday

NOTES

ACCOMPLISHMENTS
FOR THE WEEK OF _____ TO _____

Monday

NOTES

Tuesday

Wednesday

Thursday

Friday

Saturday

Sunday

"Planning to retire? Before you do find your hidden passion, do the thing that you have always wanted to do."
—Catherine Pulsifer

PLAN FOR THE WEEK OF _____ TO _____

Monday

Tuesday

Wednesday

Thursday

Friday

Saturday

Sunday

NOTES

ACCOMPLISHMENTS
FOR THE WEEK OF _____ TO _____

Monday

NOTES

Tuesday

Wednesday

Thursday

Friday

Saturday

Sunday

"We work all our lives so we can retire-so we can do what we want with our time-and the way we define or spend our time defines who we are and what we value."
—Bruce Linton

PLAN FOR THE WEEK OF _____ TO _____

Monday

NOTES

Tuesday

Wednesday

Thursday

Friday

Saturday

Sunday

ACCOMPLISHMENTS
FOR THE WEEK OF _____ TO _____

Monday

NOTES

Tuesday

Wednesday

Thursday

Friday

Saturday

Sunday

"Stay young at heart, kind in spirit, and enjoy retirement living."
—Danielle Duckery

PLAN FOR THE WEEK OF _____ TO _____

Monday

NOTES

Tuesday

Wednesday

Thursday

Friday

Saturday

Sunday

ACCOMPLISHMENTS
FOR THE WEEK OF _____ TO _____

Monday

NOTES

Tuesday

Wednesday

Thursday

Friday

Saturday

Sunday

"Establishing new schedules and routines is a great way to make the transition into retirement and help seniors find a new path forward."
—Samantha Westwood

PLAN FOR THE WEEK OF _____ TO _____

Monday

NOTES

Tuesday

Wednesday

Thursday

Friday

Saturday

Sunday

ACCOMPLISHMENTS
FOR THE WEEK OF _____ TO _____

Monday

NOTES

Tuesday

Wednesday

Thursday

Friday

Saturday

Sunday

"Retirement is still a perfectly good word, but we need to rein in its usage now that its original meaning is no longer all that relevant because people are living longer, healthier, more active lives."
—Mike Drak

PLAN FOR THE WEEK OF _____ TO _____

Monday

NOTES

Tuesday

Wednesday

Thursday

Friday

Saturday

Sunday

ACCOMPLISHMENTS
FOR THE WEEK OF _____ TO _____

Monday

Tuesday

Wednesday

Thursday

Friday

Saturday

Sunday

"...retirement is a time for personal growth, which becomes the path to greater personal freedom"
—Mark Evan Chimsky

PLAN FOR THE WEEK OF _____ TO _____

Monday

NOTES

Tuesday

Wednesday

Thursday

Friday

Saturday

Sunday

ACCOMPLISHMENTS
FOR THE WEEK OF _____ TO _____

Monday

NOTES

Tuesday

Wednesday

Thursday

Friday

Saturday

Sunday

"Once the mindless myths associated with aging are dispelled, people of traditional retirement age must learn to identify the purpose they can pursue with a passion."
—Helen L. Harkness

PLAN FOR THE WEEK OF _____ TO _____

Monday

NOTES

Tuesday

Wednesday

Thursday

Friday

Saturday

Sunday

ACCOMPLISHMENTS
FOR THE WEEK OF _____ TO _____

Monday

NOTES

Tuesday

Wednesday

Thursday

Friday

Saturday

Sunday

*"The first step to a thriving unretirement is to begin by asking yourself
what it is you want to be doing."*
—Chris Farrell

PLAN FOR THE WEEK OF _____ TO _____

Monday

NOTES

Tuesday

Wednesday

Thursday

Friday

Saturday

Sunday

ACCOMPLISHMENTS
FOR THE WEEK OF _____ TO _____

Monday

NOTES

Tuesday

Wednesday

Thursday

Friday

Saturday

Sunday

"Retirement life is different because there is not a set routine. You are able to let the day unfold as it should. Enjoy, be happy and live each day."
—Suzanne Steel

PLAN FOR THE WEEK OF _____ TO _____

Monday

Tuesday

Wednesday

Thursday

Friday

Saturday

Sunday

NOTES

ACCOMPLISHMENTS
FOR THE WEEK OF _____ TO _____

Monday

Tuesday

Wednesday

Thursday

Friday

Saturday

Sunday

"Creating your semi-retirement can be the best thing you ever do for yourself. Start by envisioning what you'd like your life to be like, if you only had more time."
—Robert Clyatt

PLAN FOR THE WEEK OF _____ TO _____

Monday

Tuesday

Wednesday

Thursday

Friday

Saturday

Sunday

ACCOMPLISHMENTS
FOR THE WEEK OF _____ TO _____

Monday

NOTES

Tuesday

Wednesday

Thursday

Friday

Saturday

Sunday

*"I'm not retiring. I am graduating. Today is my graduation day.
Retirement means that you'll just go ahead and live on your laurels an
surf all day in Oceanside. It ain't going to happen.."*
—Junior Sean

PLAN FOR THE WEEK OF _____ TO _____

Monday

Tuesday

Wednesday

Thursday

Friday

Saturday

Sunday

NOTES

ACCOMPLISHMENTS
FOR THE WEEK OF _____ TO _____

Monday

NOTES

Tuesday

Wednesday

Thursday

Friday

Saturday

Sunday

"Others will keep working because the 'gold' in our so-called 'golden years'
doesn't have to come from watching sunsets."
—Arianna Huffington

PLAN FOR THE WEEK OF _____ TO _____

Monday

NOTES

Tuesday

Wednesday

Thursday

Friday

Saturday

Sunday

ACCOMPLISHMENTS
FOR THE WEEK OF _____ TO _____

Monday

Tuesday

Wednesday

Thursday

Friday

Saturday

Sunday

NOTES

"As you embark on the exciting journey into retirement, you will experience a transition that will be both thrilling and terrifying."
—Olivia Greenwell

PLAN FOR THE WEEK OF _____ TO _____

Monday

Tuesday

Wednesday

Thursday

Friday

Saturday

Sunday

NOTES

ACCOMPLISHMENTS
FOR THE WEEK OF _____ TO _____

Monday

NOTES

Tuesday

Wednesday

Thursday

Friday

Saturday

Sunday

"No doubt excellent health is an important asset. Nonetheless, many retirees with health problems are still able to enjoy their leisure time and life in general."
—Ernie J. Zelinski

PLAN FOR THE WEEK OF _____ TO _____

Monday

NOTES

Tuesday

Wednesday

Thursday

Friday

Saturday

Sunday

ACCOMPLISHMENTS
FOR THE WEEK OF _____ TO _____

Monday

NOTES

Tuesday

Wednesday

Thursday

Friday

Saturday

Sunday

"As your life changes, it takes time to recalibrate, to find your values again. You might also find that retirement is the time when you stretch out and find your potential."
—Sid Miramontes

PLAN FOR THE WEEK OF _____ TO _____

Monday

Tuesday

Wednesday

Thursday

Friday

Saturday

Sunday

NOTES

ACCOMPLISHMENTS
FOR THE WEEK OF _____ TO _____

Monday

NOTES

Tuesday

Wednesday

Thursday

Friday

Saturday

Sunday

"Sit back and relax and do the things you never got a chance to do."
—Julie Hebert

PLAN FOR THE WEEK OF _____ TO _____

Monday

Tuesday

Wednesday

Thursday

Friday

Saturday

Sunday

ACCOMPLISHMENTS
FOR THE WEEK OF _____ TO _____

Monday

NOTES

Tuesday

Wednesday

Thursday

Friday

Saturday

Sunday

"I have never liked working. To me a job is an invasion of privacy."
—Danny McGoorty

PLAN FOR THE WEEK OF _____ TO _____

Monday

NOTES

Tuesday

Wednesday

Thursday

Friday

Saturday

Sunday

ACCOMPLISHMENTS
FOR THE WEEK OF _____ TO _____

Monday

NOTES

Tuesday

Wednesday

Thursday

Friday

Saturday

Sunday

"Just because you are getting older and have retired doesn't mean that you should have less confidence in your abilities. Think about the experience and knowledge that you have gained by all the years you have worked!"
—Theodore W. Higginsworth

PLAN FOR THE WEEK OF _____ TO _____

Monday

Tuesday

Wednesday

Thursday

Friday

Saturday

Sunday

NOTES

ACCOMPLISHMENTS
FOR THE WEEK OF _____ TO _____

Monday

NOTES

Tuesday

Wednesday

Thursday

Friday

Saturday

Sunday

"Retirement, a time to do what you want to do, when you want to do it, where you want to do it, and how you want to do it."
—Catherine Pulsifer

PLAN FOR THE WEEK OF _____ TO _____

Monday

NOTES

Tuesday

Wednesday

Thursday

Friday

Saturday

Sunday

ACCOMPLISHMENTS
FOR THE WEEK OF _____ TO _____

Monday

NOTES

Tuesday

Wednesday

Thursday

Friday

Saturday

Sunday

"Retire from work, but not from life."
—M. K Soni

PLAN FOR THE WEEK OF _____ TO _____

Monday

NOTES

Tuesday

Wednesday

Thursday

Friday

Saturday

Sunday

ACCOMPLISHMENTS
FOR THE WEEK OF _____ TO _____

Monday

NOTES

Tuesday

Wednesday

Thursday

Friday

Saturday

Sunday

"As in all successful ventures, the foundation of a good retirement is planning."
—Earl Nightingale

PLAN FOR THE WEEK OF _____ TO _____

Monday

NOTES

Tuesday

Wednesday

Thursday

Friday

Saturday

Sunday

ACCOMPLISHMENTS
FOR THE WEEK OF _____ TO _____

Monday

NOTES

Tuesday

Wednesday

Thursday

Friday

Saturday

Sunday

"Don't simply retire from something, have something to retire to."
—Harry Emerson Fosdick

PLAN FOR THE WEEK OF _____ TO _____

Monday

NOTES

Tuesday

Wednesday

Thursday

Friday

Saturday

Sunday

ACCOMPLISHMENTS
FOR THE WEEK OF _____ TO _____

Monday

NOTES

Tuesday

Wednesday

Thursday

Friday

Saturday

Sunday

"Don't act your age, in retirement. Act ike the inner young person you have always been."
—J. A. West

PLAN FOR THE WEEK OF _____ TO _____

Monday

Tuesday

Wednesday

Thursday

Friday

Saturday

Sunday

NOTES

ACCOMPLISHMENTS
FOR THE WEEK OF _____ TO _____

Monday

NOTES

Tuesday

Wednesday

Thursday

Friday

Saturday

Sunday

"Retirement has been a discovery of beauty for me. I never had the time before to notice the beauty of my grandkids, my wife, and the tree outside my very own front door. And the beauty of time itself."
—Hartman Jule

PLAN FOR THE WEEK OF _____ TO _____

Monday

Tuesday

Wednesday

Thursday

Friday

Saturday

Sunday

NOTES

ACCOMPLISHMENTS
FOR THE WEEK OF _____ TO _____

Monday

Tuesday

Wednesday

Thursday

Friday

Saturday

Sunday

NOTES

"Retirement means doing whatever I want to do. It means choice."
—Dianne Nahirny

PLAN FOR THE WEEK OF _____ TO _____

Monday

Tuesday

Wednesday

Thursday

Friday

Saturday

Sunday

NOTES

ACCOMPLISHMENTS
FOR THE WEEK OF _____ TO _____

Monday

Tuesday

Wednesday

Thursday

Friday

Saturday

Sunday

"Rest is not idleness, and to lie sometimes on the grass under trees on a summer's day, listening to the murmur of the water, or watching the clouds float across the sky, is by no means a waste of time."
—J. Lubbock

PLAN FOR THE WEEK OF _____ TO _____

Monday

NOTES

Tuesday

Wednesday

Thursday

Friday

Saturday

Sunday

ACCOMPLISHMENTS
FOR THE WEEK OF _____ TO _____

Monday

NOTES

Tuesday

Wednesday

Thursday

Friday

Saturday

Sunday

"There is a whole new kind of life ahead, full of experience just waiting to happen. Some call it 'retirement'. I call it bliss."
—Betty Sullivan

PLAN FOR THE WEEK OF _____ TO _____

Monday

Tuesday

Wednesday

Thursday

Friday

Saturday

Sunday

NOTES

ACCOMPLISHMENTS
FOR THE WEEK OF _____ TO _____

Monday

NOTES

Tuesday

Wednesday

Thursday

Friday

Saturday

Sunday

"I enjoy waking up and not having to go to work. So I do it three or four times a day."
—Gene Perret

PLAN FOR THE WEEK OF _____ TO _____

Monday

NOTES

Tuesday

Wednesday

Thursday

Friday

Saturday

Sunday

ACCOMPLISHMENTS
FOR THE WEEK OF _____ TO _____

Monday

NOTES

Tuesday

Wednesday

Thursday

Friday

Saturday

Sunday

"A lot of our friends complain about their retirement. We tell 'em to get a life."
—Larry Laser

PLAN FOR THE WEEK OF _____ TO _____

Monday

Tuesday

Wednesday

Thursday

Friday

Saturday

Sunday

NOTES

ACCOMPLISHMENTS
FOR THE WEEK OF _____ TO _____

Monday

NOTES

Tuesday

Wednesday

Thursday

Friday

Saturday

Sunday

"When a man retires and time is no longer a matter of urgent importance,
his colleagues generally present him with a watch."
—R. C. Sheriff

PLAN FOR THE WEEK OF _____ TO _____

Monday

Tuesday

Wednesday

Thursday

Friday

Saturday

Sunday

NOTES

ACCOMPLISHMENTS
FOR THE WEEK OF _____ TO _____

Monday

NOTES

Tuesday

Wednesday

Thursday

Friday

Saturday

Sunday

*"Often when you think you're at the end of something,
you're at the beginning of something else."*
—Fred Rogers

PLAN FOR THE WEEK OF _____ TO _____

Monday

Tuesday

Wednesday

Thursday

Friday

Saturday

Sunday

NOTES

ACCOMPLISHMENTS
FOR THE WEEK OF _____ TO _____

Monday

NOTES

Tuesday

Wednesday

Thursday

Friday

Saturday

Sunday

"We make a living by what we get. We make a life by what we give."
—Winston Churchill

PLAN FOR THE WEEK OF _____ TO _____

Monday

Tuesday

Wednesday

Thursday

Friday

Saturday

Sunday

NOTES

ACCOMPLISHMENTS
FOR THE WEEK OF _____ TO _____

Monday

Tuesday

Wednesday

Thursday

Friday

Saturday

Sunday

NOTES

"Retirement at sixty-five is ridiculous. When I was sixty-five I still had pimples."
—George Burns

PLAN FOR THE WEEK OF _____ TO _____

Monday

Tuesday

Wednesday

Thursday

Friday

Saturday

Sunday

NOTES

ACCOMPLISHMENTS
FOR THE WEEK OF _____ TO _____

Monday

NOTES

Tuesday

Wednesday

Thursday

Friday

Saturday

Sunday

"You are never too old to set another goal or to dream a new dream."
—C.S. Lewis

PLAN FOR THE WEEK OF _____ TO _____

Monday

Tuesday

Wednesday

Thursday

Friday

Saturday

Sunday

NOTES

ACCOMPLISHMENTS
FOR THE WEEK OF _____ TO _____

Monday

Tuesday

Wednesday

Thursday

Friday

Saturday

Sunday

NOTES

*"There comes a day when you realize turning the page is the best feeling in the world.
Because you realize there is so much more to the book than the page you were stuck on."*
—Zayn Malik

I'm so happy to see you reach your goal! Retirement holds new beginnings for you. Seek out everything that retirement has to offer you.

"Retire from work, but not from life."
—M.K. Soni

ABOUT THE AUTHOR

Hyrum W. Smith is one of the original creators of the popular Franklin Day Planner and the recognized "Father of Time Management." Hyrum is former Chairman and CEO of FranklinCovey Co. He currently serves as Vice-Chairman of the Board of Tuacahn Center for the Arts.

For four decades, Hyrum has been empowering people to effectively govern their personal and professional lives. This distinguished author, speaker, and businessman combines wit and enthusiasm with a gift for communicating compelling principles that incite lasting personal change.

Hyrum is the author of nationally-acclaimed books and presentations including The 10 Natural Laws of Successful Time and Life Management, What Matters Most, Pain is Inevitable Misery is Optional, You Are What You Believe, and the Three Gaps.

Hyrum and his wife Gail live on a ranch in Southern Utah.

CPSIA information can be obtained
at www.ICGtesting.com
Printed in the USA
JSHW061130120623
43080JS00001B/1